From Pain to Pearls

From Pain to Pearls

A 31-Day Devotional for Women

SHANA GROOMS

From Pain to Pearls: A 31-Day Devotional for Women

By Shana Grooms

Unless otherwise noted, all Scripture quotations are taken from the *Holman Christian Standard Bible*®, Used by Permission HCSB ©1999, 2000, 2002, 2003, 2009 Holman Bible Publishers. Holman Christian Standard Bible®, Holman CBS®, and HCSB® are federally registered trademarks of Holman Bible Publishers.

Scripture quotations noted *King James Version* are taken from The Authorized (King James) Version. Rights in the Authorized Version in the United Kingdom are vested in the Crown. Reproduced by permission of the Crown's patentee, Cambridge University Press.

Scripture quotations noted *New American Standard Bible* are taken from the New American Standard Bible® (NASB), Copyright ©1960, 1962, 1963, 1968, 1971, 1972, 1973, 1975, 1977, 1995 by The Lockman Foundation. Used by permission. www.Lockman.org

Scripture quotations noted *The Message* are taken from The Message. Copyright ©1993, 1994, 1995, 1996, 2000, 2001, 2002. Used by permission of NavPress Publishing Group.

Cover and interior design by Karisma Design, karisma-design.com.
Photos by Meredith Ward Photography, meredithwardphotography.com.

Published by Shana Grooms.

This book is dedicated to …

My mom—
Thank you for carrying my pain to the feet of Jesus
through your earnest prayers.

My husband, Tim—
Thank you for being my steady rock.

My boys, Gage and Nash—
May you always walk in the legacy of Jesus Christ.

My dad—
Thank you for teaching me to listen
to the Holy Spirit all of my days.

Foreword

WHAT A GREAT HONOR it is to introduce my favorite author, my beautiful friend, and an amazing alongsider, Shana Grooms. God brought Shana into my journey a little over 12 years ago in His perfect timing. She was a gift that I didn't expect, but one that I desperately needed.

Our friendship took root amidst many conversations while nursing our babies, watching our toddler boys ride stick ponies and play swordfight, and listening to our husbands play guitar in the next room. She was the perfect non-judging, sweatpants-wearing, snow-day-get-together-initiating, Easter-egg-dyeing, frozen-pizza-baking, boy-raising, easy-going, keep-me-laughing kind of friend for me. But furthermore, she was that friend that just kept me real. She didn't allow me to hide away behind my insecurities or simply remain sulky during a troublesome time.

Our friendship grew as our kids grew, and it deepened as we navigated through new trials and seasons that we each encountered. And all these years later, though (sadly) separated by a few more miles, I continue to be blessed by her friendship, her wisdom, her authenticity, and her Spirit-led living. She still sharpens me. She still keeps me real. I am just as grateful for her as when we first met.

I'm also very honored to get to introduce Shana's first book. She would be the first to say that God's fingerprints are all over it. He brought several of these writings out of times of pain and hurt, both physical and emotional. I watched Shana struggle through continuous pain, never-ending appointments, disappointing test results, losses, and emotional toils. There were questions, doubts, and many tears, but her continual seeking after God also brought restoration, healing, and opened eyes and hands to His grace.

And He brought her wisdom. You see, pearls have often been symbolic of "wisdom gained through experience." She has not allowed the pain or heartaches to be wasted, but instead she allowed them to mold and refine her. They have, in essence, become pearls of wisdom, which she has since shared so they could bring encouragement to others. And that, in a nutshell, is this book. The following pages are not just filled with tragedies or details of her pain, but rather the promises and goodness of our God. They are a collection of those lessons of wisdom.

This book showcases our God, the One who quenches our thirst in a dry land or season; the One who knows how to restore us through trials; the One who uses our thorns and weaknesses to make us more complete; the One who never stops pursuing us and drawing us to himself. And this book is a tool to spur you on toward that same great God because He wants to do those very things for you too.

Thank you for giving me a snippet of your time and allowing me to share a little about my precious friend and her book. I will close by asking God for His blessing:

Holy God, may You be exalted through these pages. May Your name be called upon. Use Your Living Word to penetrate minds and hearts. May Your Spirit comfort these readers and remind them of Your love. Please continue to shine Your face upon Shana and her family. I ask these things in the righteous and most precious name of Your Son, Jesus Christ, our Savior. Amen.

Because of Jesus,
Heidi Klump

Shana Grooms

Contents

Contents (continued)

Introduction

> Again, the kingdom of heaven is like a merchant in search
> of fine pearls. When he found one priceless pearl, he went
> and sold everything he had, and bought it.
>
> Matthew 13:45–46

LIFE CAN BE MESSY. Life can be difficult. Life can be painful. But I know I'm not the only one who knows this. It's part of being human. Experiencing the struggles in life, in a way, reminds us we are alive. It is through this struggle and often-times pain that we find beauty once again.

Christ began transforming my pain into pearls over ten years ago. My first pregnancy ended in miscarriage in 2005, which led to deep anxiety before giving birth to two amazing sons. After my second son turned one year old, I started having physical issues due to a childbirth injury in which I suffered from constant pain for almost two years, making me feel depressed. Shortly after, I miscarried again. Then, a couple years later, I began developing foot pain that has never left—even though my doctor is working on it.

But, hold on. I'm not telling you all this to be dramatic or to gain sympathy or to even explain my issues at all. I'm here to tell you how Jesus is taking my pain and turning it into pearls—and He can do the same for you.

I'm sure you've heard how pearls are made. In brief, an oyster is invaded by an irritant, so the oyster makes the "mother-of-pearl" to protect itself and transform the irritant into a beautiful pearl. Amazing!

This is what Jesus Christ is doing with my pain and what He can do with yours. Jesus, the metaphorical oyster, is taking my pain, the irritant, and turning it into something good. The pain does not feel good, but the pain is leading me on a closer walk with Him, and He is beautiful.

In Matthew 13, verses 45–46, quoted earlier, the merchant buys the one priceless pearl that he finds even though it costs him everything. Why? Because the pearl was worth it to him.

After reflecting upon this Scripture and allowing God to shape my perspective through many emotional conversations with Him, I'm now seeing that my pain is driving me toward this pearl—toward the Kingdom of God—by bringing me closer to Him through each experience. Therefore, my pain is not in vain. He has a purpose for it.

Knowing that God can have purpose in my pain brings me much hope, and I pray that it does the same for you. I know that living with, or in, pain can be tiring, depressing, and just plain hard. But please hear me when I say that God is able to take our pain and use it for His good.

Therefore, we have hope … and I know hope feels good!

I have decided to see each affliction as a chance to make a pearl. Hopefully I'll end with a strand of them. You can too, sweet ones. You can too!

Please join me in discovering the pearls of wisdom God gives as He transforms pain into pearls.

Crumbling Walls

When there is a prolonged blast of the horn and you
hear its sound, have all the people give a mighty shout.
Then the city wall will collapse, and the people will
advance, each man straight ahead.

Joshua 6:5

Do you remember the story of Joshua and the battle of
Jericho? (See Joshua 5 and 6.) God told the Israelites to march
around the city while blowing trumpets for six days and then
on the seventh to march around the city walls seven more
times while blowing trumpets and shouting. Kind of a funny
little story, isn't it? Wouldn't you expect God to send Joshua
and his army into the city with brute force and overtake the
city? Not our God. He does things His way, and it turns out
just right.

One reason I absolutely love this story is because my boys
enjoyed hearing about this when they were really small. We
would sing the song about it too, and it would be in my head
for days! Another reason I connect with this story, though, is
because I love how God took those walls down in an untraditional way. I think He still does this today.

Throughout the past ten years as I've gone through various trials, God has brought some walls down in my life. Through it all He allowed pain to produce a vulnerability in me. He allowed me to "get real," so to speak. Previously, when I had challenges that seemed to last for a while or when one ended and another sprang up rather quickly, it was easy for me to hide. I could pretend everything was going well; but pain has a way of showing that not everything is going well, no matter how hard you try to conceal it.

When I had to admit that I was weak, that I needed help, that I couldn't go to work without ever taking a sick day, my walls tumbled down. I was not able to stay encircled in my comfort zone. But praise God, He conquered my city … He conquered my heart. And He is able to do the same for you.

Now, don't get me wrong. I gave my life to Jesus Christ a long time ago, but He knew where certain parts of my heart held stone, and the Pearl Maker declared that it was time for my walls to come down. This would allow all of His desires to start running through my veins, giving me new energy, vision, and song.

I know that this process will be a lifelong one because inevitably from time to time I will try to rebuild my walls of stone. What is it that makes us scared to be exposed during our struggles? Here's what I find: When I daily surrender my heart to Jesus, He will keep turning that stone into flesh where life can freely flow.

He wants us to give Him what we have during the pain. He understands that we are possibly in a place where we feel more vulnerable than we ever have before due to our human weakness. And I can't help but think that quite possibly this place of vulnerability with Jesus is the perfect place to be. May He continue to use our pain to transform our hearts.

Juggling Time

> I am sure of this, that He who started
> a good work in you will carry it on to completion
> until the day of Christ Jesus.
>
> Philippians 1:6

Do you ever find yourself wondering if there's enough time? As a wife, mother, daughter, teacher, etc., I know I sure do. And then the juggling begins. Just when I seem to have some things safely in the air, the others are near dropping onto the floor ... or are splattered like a cracked egg in a frying pan.

Why do we worry about time so much, sweet ones? Is it because we feel it slipping away so quickly? Is it because we can't control time and it keeps moving forward? Or are we afraid we won't get accomplished what we are supposed to within a certain time frame?

I know we could talk forever about time, but I want to focus on the last worry that I mentioned: being afraid we won't accomplish our goals within a certain time frame.

Let's just pause and ask ourselves, "What time frame?" Is it our own time frame? Or are we running on the time that the

Creator of Time controls? I'm not asking this nonchalantly. I'm really asking because it's so easy for me to forget that God is in absolute control of time. So, if I'm committing my ways to Him, can't I trust that He will accomplish everything He has planned in the time He's given to me?

Wow! What a stress relief! As long as I'm focused on Him and seeking to do His will, it will be completed. Hallelujah that I don't have to worry about this one!

Are we worrying too much about what we can accomplish all at once? Or maybe it's a perspective issue in that we are asking the wrong question. Perhaps we should be asking, "What is God trying to accomplish through me right now, and am I allowing Him to lead?" In fact, I'd like to challenge you to sit with God today and ask Him that very question.

Let's stop our own juggling acts, friends, and pray. Let's take the time to talk to the Pearl Maker so that we can become the pearls He's calling us to be.

Beautiful Broken Heart

The sacrifice pleasing to God is a broken spirit.
God, You will not despise a broken and humbled heart.

Psalm 51:17

HAVE YOU EVER FOUND YOURSELF feeling like you were useless? Perhaps you've been mourning things lost. Maybe you don't feel like Super Woman because you can't tend to your home the way you had hoped. Maybe you feel bothered that you can't seem to do it all and not look like you've been hit by a tornado, or maybe you can't be that best friend to everyone because deep down inside you question your own worth.

When we are going through any type of pain or trial, why is it that we tend to offer grace to everyone else except ourselves? If you see a friend going through a struggle, you want to offer help and encouragement. But if you are the one struggling, do you find it difficult to extend that same type of merciful attitude to yourself? I used to, until Jesus taught me to see another way.

According to the words of Psalm 51:17, God does not despise my broken and humbled heart, so why should I? So many times I have felt "less than" because I was going through a struggle and couldn't seem to make everything feel OK for myself or my family. However, when I am going through some sort of pain, I now realize that the pain leads to humility because I can't do life on my own. Yes, it is so freeing to even type this: I can't do life on my own. I. Need. Jesus.

If pain during these last ten years of my life has been my "humbling block," then I praise Jesus for the pain. If God wanted me in the place where my spirit was broken, the place where I realize how much I need Him, then may I offer up my brokenness *to* Him. Only He can pull me together and take me to the place He desires for me to be. A place that is close to Him where I am loved. A place where I am not useless because I am in the hands of the Almighty Creator.

A place where He is shaping my heart in new ways I didn't even know existed.

Can He do the same for you, sweet one? Yes, He sure can. But don't wait until you have it all together because you can't fool the Pearl Maker. He loves you … even if your heart is broken right now.

Touching His Garment

> A woman suffering from bleeding for 12 years, who had
> spent all she had on doctors yet could not be healed by
> any, approached from behind and touched the tassel of
> His robe. Instantly her bleeding stopped.
>
> Luke 8:43-44

Do you know what I really think I need to say to you right now? It's something that, as I'm typing, I'm going to say out loud so that I can hear it too. It's this: Keep trustin', baby.

I do not know why I have to say some things out loud, but I do. I guess it helps to reinforce the message to my mind, heart, and soul all at the same time. I guess hearing audible advice, even from myself, sounds more convincing.

Some days, I just need to hear those simple words: Keep trusting. Today is one of those days. It's not a terrible day or anything, but my physical pain can sometimes cause me to doubt that He is still in control. I've learned to halt the doubt by reinforcing truths that I need to hear, by reminding myself that I serve The Almighty God and that I can trust Him with my life.

When I think of trusting, I often think of the woman mentioned in this Scripture passage and how she was in such need. To bleed for twelve years would be enough to drive a girl crazy. I know that some of you, along with myself, can understand the monotony of going to various doctors and appointments without much luck. In those times, a bleeding woman couldn't enter the temple because she would've been deemed unclean during that time. She not only suffered physically, but she was kept away from the place where she could sacrifice and worship.

Can you imagine her pain? Feeling as if I couldn't come close to God and others would leave me an emotional mess. How about you? I guess that's why I'm amazed, and at the same time *not* amazed, when she reaches to touch Jesus' garment. On one hand, she might've felt scared as she came close to the Son of God; but, on the other hand, she craved Him. She needed the Savior. She needed Jesus.

Has your difficulty made you crave Him? Perhaps her struggle was the only way she would truly crave Jesus, which led to her healing as she touched His garment.

Dealing with pain has pushed me to crave Jesus all the more. But sometimes, if I'm perfectly honest, I just feel worn out and want to skip right to the healing part. That's when I reflect on this story and remind myself to keep trusting Him. I want to truly crave more of Jesus.

Tonight, once again, I will pray, holding my hands up to God, reminding Him that I would gladly touch the hem of His garment. Will you join me?

All My Heart

Listen, Israel! The Lord our God, the Lord is One.
Love the Lord your God with all your heart, with all your
soul, with all your mind, and with all your strength.

Mark 12:29-30

I'VE BEEN THINKING ABOUT what this Scripture actually looks like. In everyday life, what can we do to put these words into action?

Let's start with the first part of verse 30: Love God with all our hearts. I'm not even going to begin to claim that I am capable of having all the creative forms of putting this first one into action. However, if you'll allow me, I'd like to present some ideas of what it could look like (but am in no way limiting you to my ideas).

Perhaps a woman who is in the middle of a struggle or pain can love God with her whole heart by allowing Him to know her true feelings. And maybe these feelings aren't the ones that she even wants to acknowledge are there, but the pain has her crying out in a raw way: feeling jealous after miscarrying when looking at another pregnant woman, feeling angry that she again is not healed when someone who doesn't even worship God receives healing, feeling distrustful about God's goodness. The list could go on and on.

If we are going to love God with all our hearts, don't we have to let Him in ... even when it means we show Him our ugliness? We sure do. Instead, though, we try to hide it. Maybe it's shame. Maybe it's fear. Maybe we're disgusted with ourselves. We can't fix it. But please hear me when I say to you and remind myself: Only He can handle all of this within our hearts. So, what's a girl to do?

Open. Open your whole heart. Let Him see the ugly parts. Let Him find the cobwebs that we hope are hidden. Let Him begin His work. His healing. His cleansing. Oh, the ways of the gentle Healer of our hearts.

Open your heart to Jesus. And watch your love for Him grow even more.

All My Soul

Listen, Israel! The Lord our God, the Lord is One.
Love the Lord your God with all your heart, with all your
soul, with all your mind, and with all your strength.

Mark 12:29-30

I MENTIONED TO YOU that I wanted to take this Scripture and imagine what this really looks like in everyday life when we put these words into action.

So, the focus today is the second part of verse 30: Love God with all our souls. Again, I'm not even going to begin to claim that I am capable of having all the creative forms of putting this into action. But, I have been exploring how this might look. Want to take a look with me?

Perhaps a woman who is in the middle of a struggle or pain loves God with her whole soul by being ever mindful that her life is not only *from* God, but she also realizes it is *in* God as well. This woman does not just imagine her soul as something that will later leave her body after death. Her soul is the very essence of her living being even right now. According to Carl Schultz at www.biblestudytools.com, "In the Old Testament a mortal is a living soul rather than having a soul. Instead of splitting a person into two or three parts, Hebrew thought sees a unified being, but one that is profoundly complex, a psychophysical being." Therefore, her soul is who she really is even in this moment.

So, sweet one, who are you, really? Big question, isn't it?

I think a part of loving God with all our souls is to give every ounce of our beings to Him even while we are alive on this side of eternity. Loving Him with our souls means that we acknowledge that the here-and-now goes along with the there-and-later because it's all tied to our God. Loving Him with the very essence of who we are gives us a firm foundation of not only who we are right now but who we are forever in eternity as well.

Maybe loving Him with all of our souls requires both surrendering to Him and living in Him while acknowledging that we came from Him. Realizing that He is responsible for every breath we take. He *is* our breath. Know what I mean?

Lastly, perhaps loving Him with all of our souls means that we sit down in whatever circumstances we are in, raise our hands to Him, and wholeheartedly trust. We don't just choose to submit to His will, but we acknowledge that His will has us right where we are for a reason ... for His glory ... for His purpose.

Again, I'm not saying I have a full picture of all this myself. But as I explore this concept openly with you through this writing, it brings me to a place of peace in my soul.

All My Mind

Listen, Israel! The Lord our God, the Lord is One.
Love the Lord your God with all your heart, with all your
soul, with all your mind, and with all your strength.

Mark 12:29-30

THE FOCUS OF TODAY is the third part of verse 30: Love God with all our minds. Let's examine how this might look in daily life.

Perhaps a woman who is in the middle of a struggle or pain loves God with her whole mind by redirecting her focus upon Jesus. During the middle of a struggle, sometimes it is only by sheer will that we can look to Him because everything else can seem to scream louder for our attention. What happens when we make our minds slow down in the middle of chaos while focusing on Christ?

Peace ... an unexplainable peace.

Have you ever noticed how much we have to fight for peace in our minds? It's a real battle at times if your mind is like mine. When my mind feels out of control, I often say that I have a little hamster trying to run on its wheel inside of my head. I hate this feeling because all it leads to is a downward spiral of anxiety. I have found that the best way to fight this is to stop letting my mind move toward what I fear and to run to Jesus, who fights the battle for me.

Running to Jesus and filling our minds with Scripture brings new life to our minds and souls. Beyond trusting, using our minds to learn the very Word of God is never time wasted. When His Word resonates within our minds, it can transform our hearts. Newly gained insights given by the Holy Spirit will never get old!

I'd like to leave you with a suggestion: Pray about God using your mind for His Kingdom, and allow His creativity to take form within you. I've been so surprised at some of the ideas God has given to me within this last year, and apart from Him I would've never even given most of them a thought.

What will He do with your mind, sweet one? I can't wait to find out.

All My Strength

Listen, Israel! The Lord our God, the Lord is One.
Love the Lord your God with all your heart, with all your
soul, with all your mind, and with all your strength.

Mark 12:29-30

THE FOCUS OF TODAY is the fourth part of verse 30: Love
God with all our strength. While you might picture physical
strength, I'd like to take a look at a different type of strength.

Perhaps a woman who is in the middle of a struggle or
pain loves God with all her strength by putting her love into
action by serving both God and others. Following God's leading, she decides to serve—even when things aren't so perfect
in her own world.

I think choosing to serve while experiencing pain is such a
perspective-shifter. Focusing on serving God and others takes
us outside of ourselves—outside the battle, while leaving it in
God's hands. That takes trust, but where's there's trust, sweet
one, there's true strength.

Sometimes the hardest thing to do during pain is to let it
be. To completely hand the struggle over to God, not reaching

for it to carry on our own. To trust. Only the strong can truly stick with this plan, but if we allow Him, His strength can carry us.

Serving in the midst of pain is difficult, but this could lead to such a loving cycle. Quite possibly one person who is suffering could be serving another who is suffering and so on—what a beautiful image. Isn't this what Jesus ultimately did? He suffered for humanity while serving humanity. This is strength. Beautiful strength.

I realize our physical strength will vary from time to time throughout our lives, but our willingness to offer whatever strength we do have to serve Him does not have to waver.

May we be strong ... in Him.

Waiting to Bloom

His delight is in the Lord's instruction, and he
meditates on it day and night. He is like a tree
planted beside streams of water that bears its fruit
in season and whose leaf does not wither.

Psalm 1:2–3

WAITING. IT'S HARD WHEN we're waiting uncomfortably.
It's hard waiting when we don't understand the purpose of
waiting.

As I wait for more healing, or as I have waited for healing
throughout my body in the past, I have moments when my
patience runs thin. I have moments when I wish for just a
little encouragement. I want to know that there is a reason for
the struggle. How do I find it? How do you?

I find refuge in the part of Psalm 1 that reads, "He is like
a tree planted beside streams of water that bears its fruit in
season and whose leaf does not wither" (verse 3).

Recently I stared at massive trees out my living room windows and realized that the trees closest to the stream have the
promise of rich nourishment from the water—a nourishment
that keeps the tree thriving, not just surviving. When the heat

strikes, or in our case when the struggles strike, the tree can thrive because it's living off the water. In our case, the Living Water. No matter what comes our way, we have hope in the Living Water!

Let me share a new revelation, one I believe God allowed me to see: We bear fruit *due* to the waiting season. The tree "bears its fruit in season." So, what happens when it's out of season for a particular tree? Is it useless? Does it not serve a purpose? No! It does what it needs to do: It keeps drinking from the water and *then* produces fruit at the appropriate time. During the tree's waiting season it stays close to the Water, and the Father will allow fruit to grow in His time.

He's preparing me. He's preparing you. Wait, and then after you have tasted the Living Water, you will bear fruit in season. Stay close to Him and learn the lessons. Then bloom, baby, bloom. Let Him open your life in such a way that people all around will not only see your fruits but will also smell the sweet aroma of Christ within you.

So, worry while waiting? Nah, that's not for those of us who are confident that we will bear fruit in His time. Wait near the Water … the Living Water, sweet ones—and get ready to bloom.

The Gentle Healer

He shouted with a loud voice, "Lazarus, come out!"
The dead man came out.

John 11:43–44

WOULDN'T IT BE GREAT if God would raise our Lazaruses right after we lose them? I mean, if we only had to grieve for a few days and then they came walking back into our lives, wouldn't that be wonderful?

I remember praying that God would bring life back into my womb once I was told that no heartbeat could be detected. I was completely caught by surprise when I was not going to give birth to the one I thought was thriving inside of me. I wept amid complete confusion.

God decided not to allow this baby to live on this side of eternity with me. At first, although sad, I accepted this and clung to God for peace. Then the sadness would come over me, and I would silently crumble. I had never been in this place with God—this place that felt silent, as if I were dangling in the middle of nowhere.

I had to lean on my family, who listened and encouraged me. I looked to women in my church family and other friends who had experienced the same type of loss. I had to learn to trust God in a new way ... a real way.

This took time and looked almost like a waltz, as I would move closer to fully trusting and then slide into doubt, back to fully trusting, and then doubt. But God remained patient and faithful by my side. Sometimes I did not know what to pray, so I would pray the Scriptures back to Him.

This is where the Giver of Life began to chisel at my character. He invited me to steadily walk in true belief that God is good and that I can trust Him. This seems impossible when you feel as if you are dangling in the middle of nowhere.

However, with our Pearl Maker, it *is* possible. He worked with me gently—much more gently than what I had expected. He worked with me faithfully, handling my days of grief and questioning without taking offense. He continued to use others to remind me of His goodness and that He was tending to my sweet one that I never held. I developed a relationship with Jesus that grew out of raw honesty and surrender. No part of me was "pulled together." I was a mess in the middle of a mess, but Jesus was making me whole. Weird, huh?

He continues to work in me and will do the same for you. He is such a gentle Healer.

If you are hurting, please give Him time to work in you. You won't regret it. He will not leave you in your grief. He will whisper His words of hope to you like He did to me. In His gentle whisper, hope will return.

His Glory, a Beautiful Sight

> Dear friends, don't be surprised when the fiery ordeal
> comes among you to test you as if something unusual
> were happening to you. Instead, rejoice as you share
> in the sufferings of the Messiah, so that you may also
> rejoice with great joy at the revelation of His glory.
>
> 1 Peter 4:12–13

SUFFERING. WHO WANTS IT? No one. Who is going to experience it? Everyone. Yes, I hate the fact as much as you hate reading it. Is there a silver lining around this ominous cloud that hangs over each of us at one time or another? Absolutely. In Christ, there absolutely is hope.

The verses in 1 Peter 4 do not try to hide the fact that trials and tests will come into our lives. So, why do I feel as if my foundation trembles when these events happen? I guess it's because I'm looking more at my situation than my faith. As long as my vision is upon this world, I'm going to feel rocked. However, when I look to the Rock, my wobbly knees begin to straighten as I stand my ground.

Standing alone, however, is not the ultimate goal according to verse 13. I am to rejoice as I "share in the sufferings of the Messiah." What? How am I to rejoice at a time when nothing feels right, is going right, or is even looking right? This sounds impossible until you read further.

As I share in the same type of sufferings as Jesus—pain, loneliness, rejection, heartache, etc.—I can then "rejoice with great joy at the revelation of His glory." When is His glory revealed in such a way that I can recognize it? Could it be when I'm focused on seeing Him and nothing else? Could it be that after I've looked at so much that seems dim that His light seems all the more bright?

I know there could be several ways to interpret His glory, but anything involving His glory is beautiful because He is beautiful. Does it mean that He is going to make all of my circumstances beautiful? Sadly, no; I don't think so. But does it mean that I'll find my peace in Him as I cling to His glory, the hope of eternal glory with Him, and glory deemed only through Him? Yes, I believe so.

This is getting deep, isn't it? My human heart is so conflicted as I write this because I know that the sufferings of this world will shake us all in one way or another, and it makes me desire His return even more. Can we endure the wait, sweet ones? With Him at our sides, knowing exactly how it feels to suffer everything on this side of eternity, we sure can. And we won't just endure. We will see Him and His glory shining through ... and even shining through us. Now, that's a beautiful sight.

Turn on the Light

> Life was in Him, and that life was the light of men.
> That light shines in the darkness,
> yet the darkness did not overcome it.
>
> John 1:4–5

DO YOU NEED SOME HOPE today? Maybe it's been a rough day, week, month, or year or two. Maybe you feel like you can't see anything in front of, beside, or behind you because the darkness seems overpowering.

When my youngest son turned one year old, my body seemed to fall apart. In fact, for almost a year, I tended to get sick, go to the doctor, and then repeat the cycle when I would catch something else. I remember dreading Fridays because it almost always seemed that by Friday of each week, or every other week, I was fighting something else. Needless to say, this time of my life seemed bleak.

You know how the trees look in the winter? That's how I felt on the inside: empty. Who could dream of flourishing in the middle of such moments when it felt that survival was the main goal for my little ones and me? Nothing was life-threatening, but the constant storms tattered my sails. They were threadbare.

What does a person do in the middle of a season that feels so dark? Well, sisters, don't forget to turn on the Light. Talk to your Savior, relish the light found in His Word. Sit quietly with Him and allow the Holy Spirit to intercede for You.

I am so encouraged by the fact that life exists in Christ and that He is the Light. His light shines in the deepest darkness. But here's the best part: His promise that the darkness has NOT overcome it! I'm getting excited just typing those words!

No matter what darkness we are going through, the Light shines brighter. He is bigger. He is more powerful. He is the Victor over the darkness that exists in this world.

I've got an idea. Whenever things might seem dim in your world, go turn on a light or burn a candle in your house to remind yourself that He is your Light and that He is shining in your darkness. Sound silly? Maybe it is a little, but this physical reminder might help you remember that your darkness quickly dissipates with the Light. You could even lay a strand of pearls near that light to remind you of your awesome Pearl Maker.

Praising... Always

> I will sing to the Lord all my life;
> I will sing praise to my God while I live.
>
> Psalm 104:33

DURING THE DARKEST OF DAYS do you ever find yourself praising even more? I don't mean right away or maybe as soon as you start fighting a battle, but as you go further into the war, do you find yourself singing praises to God?

Praise has been one of my lifelines. In fact, praise has been my connector to God even when I couldn't hear His voice. Worshiping God has been a way for me to not only glorify God but also to remind me of His love, His promises, and His perfection.

I love to sing, and I'm convinced that if God had made me a bird, I would've been a canary. But, unlike the canary who instinctively sings because that's what the Creator created a canary to do, I make a choice to praise with my heart and voice. I believe the Creator, or Pearl Maker, has designed me to praise Him. It's not enough that I just praise with my lips; my heart and life need to praise Him ... even when life is painful.

True commitment to my Savior pushes me to praise in all seasons of life. My praises may sound different as I undergo various circumstances. When I am in pain, my praise may sound softer than when I am not, but nonetheless, I want to praise.

I know that some of you are venturing across tough terrain right now, terrain that I cannot imagine walking through. Others of you have walked many miles in the dark, and now you are enjoying the sunshine. Either way, we are all connected. We have all experienced dark seasons. The question is this: Are you singing? If not, perhaps today you can start—not because life suddenly became easier, but because our God is worthy and He "inhabititest the praises" of His people (Psalm 22:3, *King James Version*).

Faithful in the Flame

> King Nebuchadnezzar . . . said to his advisers, "Didn't we
> throw three men, bound, into the fire? . . . I see four men,
> not tied, walking around in the fire unharmed;
> and the fourth looks like a son of the gods."
>
> Daniel 3:24–25

I LOVE THE STORY of Shadrach, Meshach, and Abednego from Daniel 3. In short, these three godly men refused to worship false gods and to only worship God himself. When they refused to bow down to idols, the king threw them into a fiery furnace. But they did not burn. In fact, they didn't even smell like smoke when they walked out! In verse 27 we read that this led the king to worship the Living God.

I want to focus today on the moment when the king looked into the fiery furnace. God sent a physical reminder of His presence to be with His faithful followers. In essence, He was willing to stand in the flame with His men. He still does the same with us.

Pain can make you feel lonely and almost ashamed. You feel like someone who always has an "issue." Although if we really think about it, aren't we all in this category? The good news: We are God's beloved. He does not forsake us.

I distinctly remember when I realized God was willing to stand in the flame with me. I was receiving an acupuncture treatment for one of my chronic issues when my youngest son was a year old and my oldest was around age three. I was spent. Physically exhausted. Emotionally drained and disheartened. As I lay there with needles in my skin, crying as I prayed, the Holy Spirit spoke encouraging words to me: "I may not take your pain away, but I'll be right beside you through it all."

Having Him beside me through years of doctor's appointments and treatments for various things has been life-changing for me. I know He offers to do the same for all of you. He is faithful in the flame of pain . . . physical or emotional.

So, why does He choose to walk faithfully beside us in the flame? One reason I have come to believe is that when He walks this close to us, He can refine us. In Psalm 66:10 we read, "For You have tried us, O God; You have refined us as silver is refined" (*New American Standard Bible*).

Now, I'm no expert on refining silver, but I do know that the refiner has to be close to the silver as it is being refined so that he can see his reflection in it. The refiner and the "refinee" are connected through this process in a way that compares to no other relationship. The silver changes until it reflects the image of the one refining it.

God takes the pain and turns it into pearls in the meta-phorical Refiner's fire. He draws us close to Him, keeping His eye directly on us while we are being refined by whatever He is using. The result is that we come out of the Refiner's fire in closer relationship with Him, with His mark and His image upon us. Others can see His mark and smell His fragrance. Is that beautiful or what?

So, if you are standing in the flame, hang in there, sweet one. He can use this time in your life to bring glory to Him because He's the ultimate Refiner.

Hearing the Whisper

And after the fire there was a voice, a soft whisper.

1 Kings 19:12

I THINK ONE OF THE HARDEST things about pain—physical or emotional—is that it sometimes brings you to a standstill. It makes you feel like you are stuck. Know what I'm saying?

There are times during the struggle when it can feel as if everyone else is moving forward by leaps and bounds and you are standing still—or even worse, lying flat on your face, in sinking sand. Not a good feeling!

Can I pose a different way of thinking about these "still moments"?

Perhaps the Lord brings us to these times of stillness so we can hear Him whisper. Could it be that when we are going at a fast pace, day after day after day, it's hard for us to notice Him? I am so totally guilty of this!

I love the Scripture that tells of the prophet Elijah going "on the mountain in the Lord's presence" (1 Kings 19:11–12).

Can you even imagine what he was expecting? The very presence of the Lord! The Scripture continues, "A great and mighty wind was tearing at the mountains and was shattering cliffs. . . . After the wind there was an earthquake. . . . After the earthquake there was a fire." However, it says that the Lord was not in any of those.

After all of these mighty things, there was a soft whisper. A. Soft. Whisper. And it was the voice of the Lord.

Wow! The God of the universe, who can thunder His way into our worlds, chooses to whisper.

If you are going through a struggle, if you are feeling stuck, join me in standing still in the mess or chaos or sorrow and *listen*. Listen for the whisper of God. Perhaps He is whispering the very hope you've been waiting to hear. You will hear from no one more convincing than our wonderful Pearl Maker.

Face Lift

You, Lord, are a shield around me, my glory,
and the One who lifts up my head.

Psalm 3:3

HAVE YOU EVER FALLEN FLAT? I don't necessarily mean physically, but emotionally? Are you dealing with a struggle that has you so emotionally exhausted that you just want to quit moving forward, quit trying to push through?

A struggle that lasts for a long while can leave you feeling like this. I've been there. I've felt like every time I take two steps forward, I always fall at least one step back (literally, with my foot issues). I live with a little hope that things are getting better, and then I feel the pain again ... *ugh*!

I have to admit that sometimes all I want to do is sit and cry. Sometimes I do just that. What makes me resolve to keep hoping and praying to the Healer when time and time again the struggle does not end? He not only gets me back on my feet, but He lifts up my head.

You might be thinking, "Well, Shana, if He gets you back on your feet, then obviously He lifted up your head." But that's exactly where I want to pause and explain.

When your child is trying to tell you that he or she is hurt and in pain, where do you look? Do you look where the child is pointing, or do you look in your child's eyes? Eyes tell us a lot, don't they? They are especially telling to someone who knows you and loves you.

This is why I think the Scripture says that God "lifts up my head." He sees the pain by looking in my eyes, so to speak. He does what any parent does when a child is hurting. He consoles me by lifting up my head because He sees that I need Him first. Then, He can take care of the pain or injury. God comes close enough to us to lift our faces because He is not only a holy God, but also a personal God.

Let our God lift your precious face while you are hurting. Allow Him to comfort you as no one else in this world can. Get close to Him. Accept how much He loves you in the midst of your pain. I can't wait to see Him lift your beautiful face as you stand once again.

The Power of an "Alongsider"

Carry one another's burdens.

Galatians 6:2

I DID NOT BELIEVE that I was a great "alongsider" until I learned that I desperately needed alongsiders in my life. An alongsider is not just a well-wisher, not even just a friend. An alongsider is someone who comes alongside of you—even when you are an absolute mess . . . someone who simply chooses to walk with you as an act of true love.

I am blessed because I have experienced the power of alongsiders. These people have seen me with my makeup smeared, my clothes mismatched, my hair unwashed, and my emotions even more distraught than my appearance. These people did not just stand at a distance and offer words of encouragement. They made the choice to step inside my world. I had nothing to offer them at the time. They walked alongside me out of love for Jesus and for me.

41

My alongsiders have made numerous phone calls, offered countless prayers, and shared many bedside moments (with my foot hooked up to a cooling machine, propped up on a bean bag, while drinking coffee with me—a very funny picture). Sometimes, we'd talk about my predicament, but mostly we just shared life by sharing time with one another. The presence of an alongsider can change a drab day or situation and make it seem at least bearable if not kind of fun—in a weird sort of way.

An alongsider doesn't have to catch up with how you are doing; she knows how you are. She's standing in the pit beside you. She's lifting you up. Then, once she gets you up and moving in the right direction, she's following right behind you because the pit is not a place where anyone should live.

How beautiful the love of Jesus looks when we allow it to live through our own skin! This, my friends, is what attracts others to Him. He is beautiful, and when we lift others up and carry their burdens, we begin to look like our Pearl Maker, Christ himself.

I'm here praying for all of my readers to consider being an alongsider to someone or to be brave enough to tell someone that you need one. If you are fortunate enough to have an alongsider in your life right now, maybe it's time to give a shout out to that person. A simple "Thank you" and cup of coffee together might be nice too.

I told you earlier that I wasn't a great alongsider, and I really wasn't. But through Christ's persistence and patience, He has made me have the desire to walk alongside others and encourage them through their pain. If you are in a struggle right now, please hear me when I say that Jesus is the BEST alongsider. He can provide other alongsiders in your life through the body, or people, of Christ.

You don't have to journey alone. He is there. May God build us up as we walk alongside one another, turning our struggles into a strong strand of pearls.

Invited, Not Rejected

> You prepare a table before me
> in the presence of my enemies.
>
> Psalm 23:5

REJECTION HURTS, DOESN'T IT? Our hearts hurt when we are rejected by others. It's hard to bear the insult, to hear about the event you were intentionally not invited to, or to see others trying to hide that they are whispering about you.

I have felt the sting of rejection. As a high school teacher I hear the phrase, "Teenage girls are so mean." This saddens my heart because anyone who is a woman today knows that yes, while teenage girls can be mean, adult women can be too.

Let's not sit in the fact that humans can be mean to one another. Let's take a step out of that brokenness and sit down at the all-welcoming table of the Father. This is where everyone is invited. I mean literally *everyone* is invited.

No one is going to pull the chair out from under you. No one is going to refuse to sit by you. No one is going to ask you to sit, only to leave you behind later. No one is going to try to leave you out of the conversation or meal.

At the Father's table, you are not only invited, but you are cherished here. He has prepared for you a specific place to sit. You were thought of long before you came to dinner. And even better, you are protected. Your heart can open, and you can be the real you. You are accepted, sweet one.

Did you hear me? You are accepted. Our Pearl Maker is focused on you as you dine with Him. Wow, can you picture that? I can, and it makes me feel so loved and relieved.

You don't have to stay in a rejected state. When, not *if*, you feel rejected, you have the choice to keep moving forward. Move forward with sisters in Christ who love you unconditionally. Move forward to Jesus who always has open arms and a place at His table. Move into your spot, friend. He's got you.

Picture This

> What matters is faith working through love.
>
> Galatians 5:6

I think that God must be taking my "word brain" and trying to expand it to a "picture brain." This is odd for me because I'm naturally a "word girl." I just love being open to Him, don't you?

I ran across this portion of Scripture in Galatians and thought that the words were beautiful. Then I started wondering how this verse might look when lived out. And for whatever reason, I imagine handholding. Not holding hands in a romantic setting, but children of God holding hands to signify help and unity.

I love the times that I have met with other women to pray. I love how we grab each other's hands as we talk to our Father. I've never really thought about it until now, but isn't our willingness to grab the hand of a sister or brother in Christ an act of faith and love? We love the Father, but we love each other too. The act of faith is praying and believing that God hears our every prayer and cares about what's on our hearts and minds. No wonder these moments are near and dear to me. I'm sure they are to you as well.

Faith works through love. So, how important is love? It is vital.

Even when I'm struggling, God is still at work within me. So, don't I still need to be working for Him—living out my faith through love? I sure do. Then it's *His* hand I'm holding, allowing me to hold my other one out to wherever He leads and to whomever He intends. Easy? Nope, especially during a trial. But beautiful? Yes, because as I'm depending on Him the most, I'm sharing Him all at the same time—not for my own glory, but for His.

At times I have desperately grasped His hand as if my next step depended on it. And now, I can thank God for the pain that drove me closer to Him. I'm so thankful that I can reach out to you through these words, sweet readers.

Keep reaching out, keep lovin', and keep workin' that faith.

Wide Open Gates

I called to the Lord in distress;
the Lord answered me and put me in a spacious place.

Psalm 118:5

I RECENTLY SAT THROUGH A DINNER with a sweet soul from my family. Her current physical battle seemed to be just too overwhelming. It was like watching a little tulip wither in front of me.

As I sat with her and saw her distress, I knew it was time. It was time to help her become unhemmed.

I don't usually focus on a word, but earlier in the year someone asked if I had to choose a word for the year what word I would choose. After much thought and saying different ones aloud, I stopped on the word *unhemmed* and its meaning of "no borders."

As I began writing this devotion, all of this seemed to come full circle. A past conversation with this loved one. A verse I began to cherish years ago. A word I had chosen to focus on. And now a current circumstance with the same loved one.

49

How do you explain to someone exactly how God has unhemmed you and your past? It's hard to go through each and every lesson learned, feeling felt, and so on. So, I took a different approach. I didn't tell her about how He brought me into a new spacious place. Instead, I decided to step over her fence and help unlock the gate.

"What fence?" you might ask. Well, you know how our minds can get when we're in the middle of a struggle. They can entrap us, making us feel as though we are behind a fence with a gate that will never open, and all we can do is run from corner to corner wondering, "How do I get out of here!?!" I could see that my loved one was running to the corners of her fence. One corner had doctors' opinions. One corner had loved ones who over-advised. Another corner had friends who remained silent because they didn't know what to say. Each corner, although not desiring to hurt, couldn't provide the real help she needed.

She needed that big gate in the fence to swing wide open so she could step out of despair and enter a spacious place. So, how does one open the gate? Put simply, sometimes we need help. When you are in pain, you may not even see an opening in the fence, no matter how big that opening is.

When I stepped over her fence, I looked for that gate … one that had been opened for me. I had no words of my own. After asking God to help me, I brought her words from Psalm 116. His Word is the best, isn't it?!

She responded quickly, and even now I'm trying to bring songs and Scripture to her each day because I know that "fence."

I also know that His Word, His Spirit working through song, and His Spirit working through others are some of the beautiful ways that God can open that gate. Sure, I can encourage the unlocking, but God swings the gate open wide so that the captive becomes unhemmed.

And oh, the feeling of that freedom—whether you run out of or stumble from that entrapment, it feels good.

He will see *her* through. He will see *you* through.

Unlock that gate by asking someone to help you, or unlock it with Christ's help, and watch the door swing wide open . . . into spacious places.

Warrior Tears

I keep the Lord in mind always.
Because He is at my right hand, I will not be shaken.

Psalm 16:8

So, I'M SITTING WITH MY FAMILY watching an episode of "American Ninja Warrior," and I find myself near tears. Yes, you heard me right: tears coupled with one of my favorite "boy-mom" shows. Let me explain.

One of the contestants lost part of his leg due to an accident and decided to not let that keep him from competing in the "American Ninja Warrior" contest. For those of you who might not be familiar with this television show contest, it requires all contestants to complete different physical challenges in order to successfully reach the end of the course. It is not an easy feat, making it all the more enjoyable to watch as you cheer on each person and hope he or she doesn't fall before advancing to the next phase. So, for this young man to rise to the challenge of even attempting this course with a prosthetic leg is nothing less than admirable.

The part that got me? When the camera showed the contestant's father. His father was teary-eyed. It was obvious that he was fighting back emotion while trying to stay focused on his boy. The father's face held stern yet tender pride as he watched his son overcome not only the obstacles in front of him but all of the ones that had come before. I'm confident that this young man's father had been by his son's side through all the dark days that had led to this shining one.

I could not help but compare the look of that father to that of our Father. Deep down in his gut the father rooted for his boy to keep going forward, to keep overcoming, to keep his eyes forward as the father inwardly ran the obstacle course beside his son. Picturing this still gets to me and makes me feel that little lump in my throat. Know what I mean?

We must not forget that our Father roots for us as we undergo the pressures of life, as we endure pain, and as we encounter trials. While God is awesome as our Creator, Redeemer, and Lord of Lords, He is also so relational. Just as the father of the contestant wouldn't dare take his eyes off his boy as he was overcoming challenge after challenge, God keeps His steady gaze upon you, sweet one. You are not forgotten. You are not overlooked. You are His.

Even though the contestant slipped and fell and didn't win the contest, you wouldn't have known it by looking at his dad's face. Sure, his dad saw him fall right then, but he had also witnessed a brave new beginning for his boy.

Nothing is too big for our sweet Jesus, nor is anything too small. His eyes are on you, kid. And that's how I know we're going to keep moving forward together.

Tennis Shoes and Pearls

> Man does not see what the Lord sees,
> for man sees what is visible,
> but the Lord sees the heart.
>
> 1 Samuel 16:7

I'VE GOT A FUNNY LITTLE STYLE going on right now. While I undergo treatment for chronic plantar fasciitis, no matter what and no matter where, black, New Balance tennis shoes are always on my feet. And yes, it's driving me a little crazy.

I want to wear boots so badly with my leggings, especially when I go to work. But nope, while I wait for the healing, I must adhere to my doctor's tried and true wisdom.

Do you ever find yourself in a situation that you so desperately want to be changed, but you have to wait? Not only do you have to wait, but you can't even look and feel the way you want to during the waiting. I mean, wouldn't you rather just pretend that everything is going really well and that you always have it all together and make it look as though waiting is no big deal? It's funny how God won't let us do this for very long, isn't it?

Yes, I'm the crumbled cookie in the cookie jar ... in pieces all at the bottom. But, you know what? I think that's when the Pearl Maker can do the most with me—when I am crumbled, pliable, and a little out of sorts ... when I know that things aren't perfect even if I want them to appear that way.

God is not into mere appearances. He's into the nitty gritty work of shaping, shifting, and contouring the parts of our hearts that need His light the most. He's into making the imperfect whole through Him. As His beloved, sometimes I think that He leaves me in tennis shoes for a while longer just to remind me that I need Him. Even in my tennis shoes, my Pearl Maker still offers to adorn me in His pearls of love.

You see, sweet ones, none of us has it all together all the time because our hearts constantly need to be tended. Fortunately, when we open our hearts to God, He cleans the corners that are dusty and not quite right yet.

So, I'm going to keep walking in my tennis shoes and pearls, knowing that while I might look a little funny right now on the outside, God is cleaning up my heart. That's always in style. Want to hit the runway with me?

This Leads to That

> But we also rejoice in our afflictions,
> because we know that affliction produces endurance,
> endurance produces proven character,
> and proven character produces hope.
>
> Romans 5:3–4

Do you ever find yourself wondering what God is up to while you are in the middle of a battle? Have you ever feared that maybe He was doing nothing? I can answer yes to both questions. However, I think these verses from Romans have helped me to take a look at what God is doing, and yes, it is something.

Do you remember that childhood song about the old lady who swallowed a fly, and then she swallowed something else to catch the fly, and the list goes on and on? These Scripture verses remind me of how one thing results in something else being done, or in this case, cultivated.

So, we start with rejoicing. When? In our afflictions? True struggle exists in afflictions, but Romans explains why we can rejoice. Affliction produces endurance.

I'm no runner, but I'm pretty sure if I were to ever run, I'd rather sprint. I'd rather start, go fast, and get finished quickly. The endurance runners amaze me because they learn to pace themselves so that they don't have to stop to catch a breath; they can simply keep steadily running.

God has had to teach me a thing or two about endurance. One, that steadiness only occurs when I'm focused on Him in front of me. Two, this is not my nature, but He can cultivate it in me if I let Him. I'm confident He can do the same for you.

Next, endurance produces proven character. Proven character is deep-rooted, isn't it? People with proven character do not sway in the wind; they stand firm. The hurricanes of struggles do not tear down proven character. While the branches may bend, they do not break.

Proven character only can come after enduring over time. Can proven character come about in a sprint? No, I'm afraid not. If only!

Then, proven character produces hope. Hope in ourselves? Nope. True hope only comes through God. After enduring pain, heartache, trial, or struggle, a person who has endured and gained proven character is wise enough to know that hope does not lie in the heart of a human soul. Hope lies in Jesus Christ alone—the cultivator of our joy, endurance, character, and hope.

I wish so badly that once we got to the place of hope that we could simply be given a medal that says, "This lesson is learned, so she will not have to do this again." But you and I both know that this is a lifelong process.

When one affliction is over, eventually we will be faced with another, and the process begins again. Is this something to dread? No, because we are going to end at a place of real hope. A place of hope that the world does not always recognize, but we do.

We will find joy in our afflictions because they lead us to our Pearl Maker, our hope.

The Anxious May Rest

Rest in God alone, my soul,
for my hope comes from Him.

Psalm 62:5

Do you ever just need a breather? A chance to sit and simply inhale and exhale, inhale and exhale, and so on? Not rapidly; just steadily.

I'm sure we all do. As I write this, it is summer. I need to intentionally create space for rest. This is hard for me to do because I love being around people, being involved in many things. During the summer when I have my break from teaching high school language arts, I have become increasingly aware of the need for rest and for making sure I take this breather while I can.

Sometimes, I can catch my mind racing with "to do" lists, or even worse, worries that I'm not doing enough, being enough, and producing enough. If any of you has ever dealt with anxiety, I think you know what I'm talking about. My downward spiral is often due to overthinking while I have the time to think. (Kind of weird, right?)

What's a girl to do when she feels like she's supposed to take a so-called breather but can't due to her anxious mind tangling her all up inside?

That's when this verse becomes alive to me: "Rest in God alone." Notice it doesn't say to just *rest* but to rest in God.

The pain of anxiety may not leave its visible mark, but it can sure make a girl fight inwardly. I find that when I just try to rest, my thoughts can lead me to doubts, insecurities, and fears that God never intended for me. But when I choose to rest in God, I'm choosing to sit down and soak Him in.

I begin to bask in what He says about me in His Word: that I am loved, I am redeemed, I am forgiven. I begin to pray and open up to Him—really leaning in to trust Him. I find myself noticing my own breath from the One who gives it to me daily. The soft inhale and exhale that sustains me comes from the Sustainer himself. Then, and only then, can I begin to truly rest.

Sweet one, if you are struggling with anxiety right now, I encourage you to rest in the fact that God won't leave you there. He may lead you to seek help in a variety of ways, but He can quiet that precious heart of yours. Take it one breath at a time.

Papaw's Wisdom

Teach a youth about the way he should go;
even when he is old he will not depart from it.

Proverbs 22:6

I STARED INTO THE ALL-KNOWING EYES of my Papaw Wilson as we sat today and talked at his kitchen table. My boys and I were there to visit him after his hospital stay. Papaw's been through a lot lately with his health, and he will quickly remind me that he is now 85 years old. He recently got home from the hospital and had quite a battle during his stay. Papaw sees the wear and tear on his physical body, and he doesn't like it. Can't blame him.

While he was talking to me, Papaw mentioned how God had really blessed him because he was not in any pain while he was in the hospital. And there it was—the wise perspective and vantage point that I've become accustomed to hearing from him since I was a little girl.

Papaw never had any daughters of his own. But he sure has loved his granddaughters (and grandsons) well. He never failed to be there for us no matter the need, and he's the first one to notice when something is not quite right. Even today, he started off the conversation asking whether my day at school had gone OK. He could sense it had been somewhat of a trying week for me (as a high school language arts teacher), even though I was trying to focus on him not me. He just can't help himself. He just knows.

Papaw has been concerned about his flesh failing in different ways. He has worried that with his passing strength, perhaps he's not the man he once was. He even said a couple times today that things just weren't ever going to be the same. I could feel that he had come to terms with this, so to speak. Then we started talking about Jesus and the hope He brings.

God offers renewed strength found only in Him. He offers help when we need it most. He offers to walk beside us each step of the way.

As Papaw breathed his oxygen and looked me straight in the eye, he proclaimed the hope we have knowing that this world isn't all there is.

Sometimes I wonder whether Papaw thinks that since his physical strength is declining, he is no longer strong and maybe he doesn't have quite as much to offer. But oh, if he could just glance through my eyes for just a moment . . .

He's taught me that marriages can last a lifetime. He's taught me that raising two sons can be extremely rewarding. He's taught me that hard work is the only type of work to do. He's shown me that when you take time to really listen, you look someone in the eyes in order to see what's really going on in their hearts. He's taught me to never rush into judgment.

He's demonstrated that pointing your finger while talking makes someone know that you're making a point that should not be ignored. He's shown me that all people matter, no matter their social status, gender, or age. He's shown me that a hug is always called for. And Papaw has shown me how to love my own by loving me. And this list could go on and on.

So, if you're reading this and you feel that you don't have much to offer—whether older or younger—please know that you do. Pain, age, or circumstances do not control what Christ can do through you. You can always point another to Christ, and that pointed finger is never wasted. Just ask my Papaw Wilson.

A Blessed Life

If you understand what I'm telling you,
act like it—and live a blessed life.

John 13:17, *The Message*

HAVE YOU SEEN THOSE DECORATIVE farmhouse-style signs that say stuff about being blessed? They say things like, "Farm Life, the Blessed Life," "Messy, Blessed Life," "Blessed, Not Stressed," or just "Blessed." I love those vintage-looking signs and have to stop myself from hanging them above every single doorway in my house. I think it's safe to say that I'm not alone in this. We all want to feel blessed. Maybe that's why I'm so drawn to the signs.

But how can a girl feel blessed, especially during the really difficult times?

Lately, I've watched my Mamaw Wilson desperately miss my Papaw, who went on to be with Jesus just a few months ago. When I talk to her, she will often say that she doesn't know what her purpose is right now without him by her side.

Even though her faith reminds her that there *is* purpose, at times her grief speaks louder.

Recently, Mamaw, my mother-in-law, and I were discussing the Bible passage where John describes Jesus washing His disciples' feet. We talked about all the things that Jesus teaches us through this example that goes much further than washing feet. I stumbled upon this passage in my reading tonight and noticed verse 17. I mean *really* noticed.

Sweet, sweet Jesus washed the feet of His disciples. The King of Kings bent down, washed those feet, and dried them on His apron (as translated in *The Message*). He got close. He got involved in helping rid His beloved followers of the dirt and grime of life. He dried their feet with a garment that was draped upon Him, much like a mother would do with her own baby. This image kind of makes me want to sit here and cry a little bit.

How often, especially during a struggle or trial, do we long for someone to get close and care for us like we are truly family? How often do we long for someone to not wince at our dirt and grime but reach in and help wipe it away? How often do we want to cry out for someone to sit close enough during our pain so they can reach out with a compassionate touch? This is exactly the type of Savior we long for ... and exactly the Savior we have.

Now, back to verse 17, the *Aha* moment for me. When we do the same as Jesus did, we will be blessed. Not just a "farmhouse sign" type of blessed. A true God's-Word-says-it type of blessed.

I saw my Mamaw live this out while Papaw was here—loving him, serving him, and literally giving him his farewell washing, including those precious feet of his. But she won't stop there. She will continue to "wash the feet" of her family and friends, still living with purpose even on days when she doesn't even realize she's doing it.

My challenge to myself, and to you, sweet ones, is to approach this week looking for ways to wash the feet of those around you. Be a blessing and receive yours.

Closer Than a Brother

> But there is a friend who stays closer than a brother.
>
> Proverbs 18:24

HAVE YOU EVER BEEN in a crowd yet felt lonely? Or maybe you're surrounded by friends, but you still feel lonely? Isn't it weird how that can happen?

I grew up as the older sister to two brothers. While both would not deny that I was the bossy older sister, they also knew that I would take care of things when needed. Now, at this stage in my life, I've seen the "protector" come out in them a time or two when it came to defending their older sis. This came as a somewhat unexpected, yet pleasant, surprise. Why? Simply because I knew that they were there for me. It did not matter to them that I had bossed them around in the past, played pranks on them while babysitting, or made them help me carry my saxophone to the bus stop. They have decided to stand right by my side.

Isn't this what we all long for when we struggle emotionally or physically? We want to know that someone is right there with us. We are not forsaken. We are not forgotten.

That's why I love this verse from Proverbs that reminds us that Jesus Christ sticks even closer to us than a brother. That's close, sweet ones. I'm reminded of how close when I see how my own two brothers are willing to stick to me (even while rolling their eyes when we're TOO close).

This gets me back to my first question about feeling lonely even when people are around. During my miscarriages, I struggled with both emotional and physical pain. I felt alone in a crowd. Though the Lord blessed me with people who supported me during that journey, nothing could ever compare to His presence.

While lying there waiting to get various needle pokes, Jesus was close. When hearing that I would have to have another procedure, He was there. When I would drive down the road, praising and crying, He sat in my front seat. And now, during this period of less physical pain, He is standing in the victory He has created . . . right there with me.

So, sweet ones, no matter if you're just feeling alone or you really are alone, remember this: Jesus sticks CLOSER than a brother. Take it from me, when it comes to living with brothers, I had a front row seat. Jesus is *really* close!

Chipped and Treasured

"For My thoughts are not your thoughts, and your ways
are not My ways." This is the Lord's declaration.
"For as heaven is higher than earth, so My ways are higher
than your ways, and My thoughts than your thoughts."

Isaiah 55:8–9

I'VE FOUND MYSELF SAYING, "This is a blessed week" more than
once, and it's only our first full day on vacation at the Outer
Banks in North Carolina. I've been excited to spend the week
with sweet souls in my family in one beach house—enjoying
the laughter, the old stories, and the new ones being made
with my own children as we carry out family traditions here.
I've also looked forward to something more this year.

I could not wait to view the grace-filled moments through
a different lens—one that was waiting to capture what God
was trying to show me as I prepared to write this week. Not
that God's inspiration isn't constantly around us as we breathe
in the very breath He gives us ... as we take in the wonder of
His creation. But to take a moment to pause, breathe Him in
even closer, and to take time to reflect.

So, here goes my first observation ...

My soon-to-be twelve-year-old son loves to gather sea-shells. It's something innately interesting to him. What's funny is that he sees so many different shells as true treasures as he hunts, finds, chooses, and stores. Often, he chooses the broken ones along with the whole ones. He really does like each of them for their uniqueness—broken chips and all. This fact might seem surprising at first because he often is an aspiring perfectionist and only wants things that seem to be just right, so to speak. So, what is it that makes him able to accept all the different seashells? I think this is the mark of the Creator in him. Just as God can see beauty in all different types and shapes of things—the broken and the unbroken—I think God has somehow worked this into my son as he pursues this hobby that he loves.

OK, so what does this have to do with anything other than a mom liking to watch her kid enjoy the beach? Well, here it is ...

In our lives when something seems broken, chipped, or imperfect, God can see something beautiful forming. As the Scripture in Isaiah reminds us, God's ways and thoughts are not limited to our ways of thinking. His are higher. His thoughts aren't even near being inside a box (or a shell, in this case). I think that's an amazing way to pause and look at our current situations.

To trust Him, knowing that He sees us in current cir-cumstances—whether chipped or worn—and reaches down to choose us from the sand, calling us His beloved, is a beautiful thing. It breathes purpose within us, no matter what we've been through, are going through, or will go through.

He chooses you, sweet one, from the sand every time.

The Raft of Surrender

Commit your way to the Lord.

Psalm 37:5

A FUNNY LITTLE INCIDENT occurred during our day today while vacationing at the beach. As my family and I took a breather from the sun and sat under our canopy, we watched a man set out to conquer the waves in an inflatable raft. While watching, we doubted this would work.

As he attempted to go beyond where the waves crashed into the shore, he clung to the side of his inflatable. We thought the waves were going to get the best of him, but he kept going until he went beyond the crest and was able to get inside the raft.

Next, he paddled, and he paddled, and he paddled. However, he never did make it out any further than where he had begun; he only drifted to the right. Even though we felt sorry for him, we also found it somewhat funny. He tried so hard. He kept paddling until he snapped his paddle apart (which they are designed to do), put one in his raft, and finally threw his hands up in surrender. At this point, we didn't blame him!

When he finally stepped out onto the sand, he seemed to begrudgingly grab the raft's handle and drag it to his spot.

This little incident made me think about all the times that I have tried to swim against the current of where God was leading me. Or maybe I was neglecting to listen to what He was trying to tell me. Or perhaps I was misplacing my focus yet again.

These situations all end at the same place: a place of frustration that leads to a place of surrender. Why is it so hard to get there sometimes? Especially when riding the waves to God's surrender is so much easier! Perhaps we think we know what's best. Maybe we think our plans would be best. Then we end up snapping our paddles apart in frustration.

Let's stop doing that. Want to? I sure do! I think I'm going to begin by really taking a look at what I'm trying to do on my own instead of with God. Then, I'm going to take that to Him and raise my hands in the inflatable raft of surrender. You with me?

Roughly Beautiful

Now the earth was formless and empty, darkness covered
the surface of the watery depths, and the Spirit of God
was hovering over the surface of the waters. Then God said,
"Let there be light," and there was light.

Genesis 1:1–3

IT WAS AN EXTRAORDINARY SCENE. A butterfly kite flying
from someone else's perch, my loves throwing frisbee in the
sand in front of me, and the ocean doing its "thing." Oh, how
it was doing its thing!

As soon as I looked out the beach house windows while
vacationing with my family, I could tell that the waves were
different today than they were yesterday. The crash was more
ferocious, heavier, and even louder. The water was showing off
its untamed nature today.

But my, oh, my how beautiful it was ...

Have you ever noticed that the roughest of waters create
the most beautiful waves? The caps show off their elegant yet
boisterous white, and the foam then contrasts with the sand as
it covers your toes and looks like froth atop a perfect latte. (I
am a true coffee lover, you must know.) The water even shows

its various shades of blue with hints of teals and lighter shades every now and then.

These moments made me reflect on God's message of hope for us: Even our toughest times—bringing ferocious, heavy, and even loud circumstances—can bring us to a place of more beauty than ever before. Is it because we are so good at cultivating the beauty from the frightening moments or even dark ones? Nope. It's just because our Creator has His way with all things—bringing order to chaos, making everything from seemingly nothing, and altering brokenness into wholeness once again, just as the beginning of His Word explains. It's His thing, sweet ones. This vision of nature made me remember that He does the same in our lives and hearts.

May you remember that even when you feel like you're in the middle of crashing waves right now, God can turn this scene into the most beautiful one yet. Hold onto your boogie boards, girls, and enjoy the foam.

Rainbow Patch Promise

Jesus Christ is the same yesterday, today, and forever.

Hebrews 13:8

OUR GOD MAKES THINGS FUN, doesn't He? While vacationing at the beach, God allowed me to remember His promises.

Have any of you seen a rainbow patch in the clouds? Until yesterday, I had not. Let me explain: You see all the rainbow colors in a perfect little stripe in the clouds but have no idea where the other end is or even where the arc is at that point. While my family and I spent time on the beach, we saw the most perfect rainbow stripe right over our blanket—not a little to the left or a little to the right, but dead center. I loved it!

His promises are real. His promises follow us. He loves to remind us of His promises.

When I looked at that rainbow stripe, I of course was reminded of God's promise to never again destroy the earth with a flood, but I was reminded of much more. I was reminded of His never-ending faithfulness. I was reminded that God wants to communicate with us, His "kids." And I was reminded of His constant presence no matter the circumstances and no matter whether or not we see Him.

The rainbow was a gift from God at just that moment, a visible reminder of an ever-present God that we can't physically see...yet.

Are any of you in a struggle, a battle, or some type of pain where you need to be reminded that God is, in fact, present—even if you don't see the rainbow right now? I've been there, sweet one. I guess that's what I think is so special about that little rainbow patch in the sky. It was a personal, physical reminder that God is still in control of anything, good or bad, in my life. He is there with you too—no matter what. Now, that's a promise to claim as true, right?

While I'm thankful for the visible reminder that God is the same God yesterday that He is today, I know some of you need to be reminded of this right now. If you don't see a rainbow patch in the sky, I'm praying that God shows you some visible reminders that you will recognize and claim as His promise to you, sent to you directly from our Pearl Maker.

Follow
Pain to Pearls
on Facebook!

www.facebook.com/shanagrooms4christ

www.ingramcontent.com/pod-product-compliance
Lightning Source LLC
LaVergne TN
LVHW052036080426
835513LV00018B/2345